Published by
North Atlantic Books
P.O. Box 12327
Berkeley, California 94712

Cover art and design by Ruby Roth
Book design by Ruby Roth

Printed in Singapore

Vegan Is Love: Having Heart and Taking Action is sponsored by the Society for the Study of Native Arts and Sciences, a nonprofit educational corporation whose goals are to develop an educational and cross-cultural perspective linking various scientific, social, and artistic fields; to nurture a holistic view of arts, sciences, humanities, and healing; and to publish and distribute literature on the relationship of mind, body, and nature.

North Atlantic Books' publications are available through most bookstores. For further information, visit our website at www.northatlanticbooks.com or call 800-733-3000.

Library of Congress Cataloging-in-Publication Data

Roth, Ruby.
  Vegan is love : having heart and taking action / written and illustrated by Ruby Roth.
    p. cm.
  ISBN 978-1-58394-354-0
  1. Animal welfare--Juvenile literature. 2. Captive wild animals--Moral and ethical aspects--Juvenile literature. 3. Veganism--Juvenile literature.
  I. Title.
  HV4708.R684 2011
  179'.2--dc22
                                              2011011444

Printed and bound by Tien Wah Press (Pte) Ltd, January 2012, in Singapore. Job #13402.

1 2 3 4 5 6 7 8 9 TWP 17 16 15 14 13 12

Vegan Is Lve

Having Heart and Taking Action

Written & Illustrated by

Ruby Roth

North Atlantic Books
Berkeley, California

How wonderful that at this very moment every person, big and small, has the power to create a better world! We don't have to wait to grow older, for laws to change, or for presidents to be elected. We can begin right now.

We can choose to live without using animals for food, clothing, or fun. As vegans, we live this way because it is best for our health, for animals, and for the earth…and *that* is love.

Many people know that animals around the world are treated badly, yet they turn their minds away. To be vegan means to care deeply about how our choices help or harm animals, how we create peace or suffering in the world.

Our choices are powerful.

Vegan is love.

Living with Love
Clothing

We love to dress in spots and stripes that make us look like animals. Fur, feathers, and scales are beautiful too, but only on the animal that wears them. Today, we can put on natural and man-made materials instead of animal parts.

There is no harmless way to use the skins of animals. Their bodies belong to them just as our bodies belong to us.

Animal Testing

Animals are often used in labs to test shampoos, soaps, cleaning supplies, and more. Some are stolen from the wild and most get ill or die in the experiments. But it doesn't have to be this way. If we stop buying these products, companies will get the message and stop experimenting on animals.

With our dollars, we can show the world what we care about. Cruelty-free products have signs like these:

NO ANIMAL INGREDIENTS

NO ANIMAL TESTING

Zoos

The zoo might be exciting, but for whom? Not the animals. There is nowhere to run, hunt, forage, or drink from rivers. Trapped, the animals grow sad, sick, and angry.

A zoo can never replace life in the wilderness.

Animals belong to this earth just as we do.

Sea Parks and Aquariums

Marine parks say they offer a fun way to learn about wild animals. But how can we learn from prisoners in a pool?

In the wild, orca whales live in huge families called pods. They are deep divers who swim up to one hundred miles per day. But to be a whale in a marine park would be like spending your life alone in a space the size of a bathtub.

Wild animals are meant for life in the wild. To keep them free, we do not visit these parks.

The Circus

You do not have to be an expert to know that animals do not want to balance on balls or jump through hoops of fire. But circus animals have to perform tricks whether they like it or not. If they don't, they are tied up or beaten with sticks, whips, and hooks.

The cheerful ringleader does not fool us. We will not see his show.

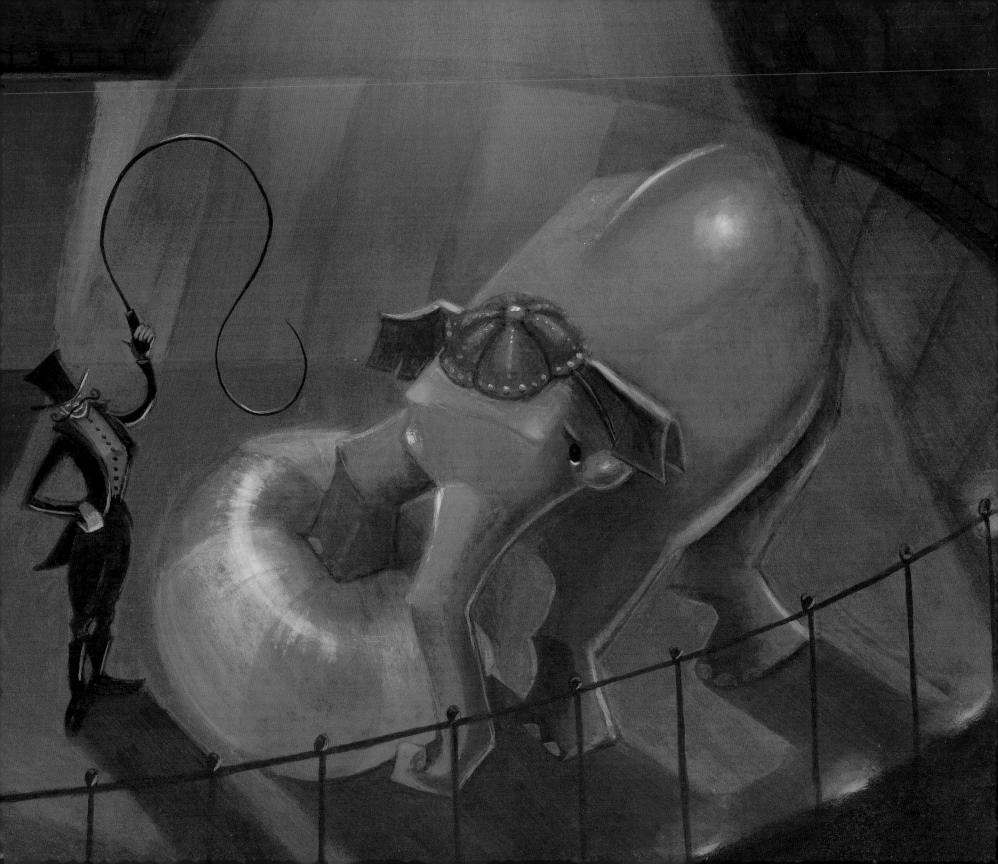

Racing

For animals, racing is loud, scary, and dangerous. Many animals are injured or killed. When they can no longer run, they are left at shelters, sent to slaughterhouses and labs, or put to death.

If we share what we know, people won't take part in hurting animals.

Hunting

Today, most hunters prey on animals because it makes them feel courageous and powerful. But killing an animal is not brave—it is cowardly. What we need today are people with the courage to protect animals, not hurt them.

Bullfights and Rodeos

When people use animals and call it a game, contest, or sport, they forget that animals are living beings with feelings, families, and instincts.

As vegans, we do not pretend that live animals are toys.

We prefer to be entertained by creatures who love to perform.

Eating with Love

Health

The truth is, we do not *need* to eat meat or dairy. Most animals in the world are herbivores, and just like them, we can grow strong and healthy by eating from nature's gardens. This way, our bodies do not collect the chemicals, fat, and disease found in animal products. Instead, we feed our bodies with love and life.

Today, being vegan is a healthier way to live.

Do No Harm

Still, some people feel good about eating meat and dairy if the animal had a nice life on a farm nearby.

But whether they live in the sunshine or in a dark shed, all animals raised for meat and dairy are captured and killed in the end. Their deaths are violent and sad.

As vegans, we do not bring the pain and suffering of any animal into our happy, healthy bodies.

Pollution

Animal farms create more pollution than all the world's cars, ships, trains, and planes put together. These farms use pesticides to kill bugs, hormones to make the animals grow terribly big, and toxic drugs for the sick—and they leak *tons* of animal poop, too.

The poisonous pollution travels thousands of miles, leaving rivers without fish, gardens without birds, and once-colorful reefs dry and white. With all this pollution, eating animals has even changed our weather.

This way of eating has been a mistake.

Organics

Raising plants instead of animals is gentler on the earth. Organic farmers treat their fields like family and care for them naturally—without chemicals or causing suffering.

By growing a garden or buying organic food from local farmers, we protect the environment and the bugs, birds, and bees who help our crops bloom. We take care of the earth so it takes care of us.

This is the healthy way to use farmland.

People

The world grows enough grain to feed everybody…but not everyone eats. Why?

Every year, the grain is used to feed sixty-five billion animals raised for meat and dairy instead of the one billion people in the world who are starving. Today, big companies are taking over people's land to build even more animal farms and raise grain to feed them.

To these companies we say, "No." A vegan way of eating uses less land and water, leaving more to share with others. Our love reaches across the world, so everyone may live free from pollution and hunger.

Forests

We choose a way of eating that does not turn forests into cattle farms or polluted fields of grain.

We are protectors of the jungles and swamps, of wild and endangered species, and of the breath of the earth.

Our love reaches from river bottoms to the highest treetops.

Oceans

For billions of years, the sea was full of life. But today, fishing has killed off much of the ocean. Fishermen continue to catch and sell what's left even when it's against the law.

It's hard to imagine that eating a little fish could harm nature. But to get just *one* fish onto a plate, a fishing boat's nets destroy miles of ocean floor, killing everything in their path.

Free from fishing, the ocean may heal and thrive over time. As vegans, our love reaches deep into the oceans.

The Arctic

With a cooler and cleaner planet, we will
protect sea ice from melting and wildlife
from disappearing. Families will not lose
the land beneath their paws.

Our love reaches to the ends of the earth.

At breakfast, lunch, and dinner, at the store or in school, we remember our love for animals. They are part of our everyday lives, part of our hearts. When we see them, we can feel them and know that we are here together—living, breathing, eating, playing, and loving under the sun.

In the end, only you can choose how to eat and live. It takes courage to ask, "What kind of person do I want to be?" and decide the answer yourself. The choice to be vegan is especially brave. It means you are standing up for yourself and all other living beings—and *that* is love.

Our choices are powerful.

Vegan is love.

What Else Can We Do?

- Connect with Animals: Never buy animals from pet stores or breeders. Rescue, visit a wildlife sanctuary, or volunteer at a local animal shelter instead.

- Activism: Write letters to companies and leaders suggesting how they could better help animals and the environment.

- Shopping: Ask your favorite grocery and clothing stores to carry more vegan products.

- Make It Yourself: Learn some vegan recipes (for food or even soaps and lotions) and share them with family, friends, and teachers.

- Home: Make your yard a sanctuary. Hang a birdfeeder or plant flowers for the bees.

- Environment: To protect animals and their habitats from pollution, replace plastic with cloth bags and glass containers.

- Gifts: Sponsor a rescued animal in your friend's name. (You can even "adopt" an elephant!)

- School: Help your school become more vegan-friendly—in the classroom and cafeteria, on field trips, and by using books like this one. Use free assignments and science fairs to learn and share more about the environmental and health benefits of veganism.

- Giving: Start a coin-collecting contest at school. The winning classroom donates all the funds to the sanctuary, animal shelter, or animal rights group of their choice. (Note: Before you choose a wildlife or "conservation" group, make sure it doesn't support hunting—some of them do!)

- Fun: Enjoy art, music, and theater shows starring people, *not* animals.

Visit www.VeganIsLove.com for more ideas and helpful links.